Scriptures taken from the HOLY BIBLE, NEW LIVING TRANSLATION,
Copyright © 1996, 2004, 2007 by Tynsdale House Foundation.
Used by permission of Tynsdale House Publishers, Inc.,
Carol Stream, Illinois 60188. All rights reserved. Used by permission.

E.R. Violet Publishing
West Des Moines, IA 50266
violetpublish@gmail.com

Printed in the United States of America

Illustrations by Bill Love

Book Design by WORD**ART**, West Des Moines, IA

This book belongs to

_____

(A child of God)

Pastor Pickle

and the LET'S GO! Club

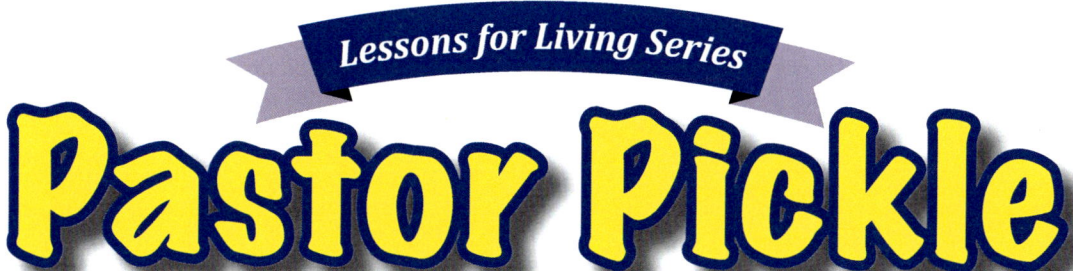

Bill & Lona Love

One day Pastor Percy Pickle and his dog, Doogie, were walking toward Pioneer Park, enjoying the birds singing their morning songs. As they cut across the church lawn, Pastor Pickle saw a young boy sitting on the edge of the fountain in the park.

"Good morning, Tommy Tipple!" Pastor Pickle said as he arrived at the fountain. He noticed Tommy Tipple was chewing on a candy bar and holding a soda in his other hand. "Enjoying this beautiful summer weather, are you?"

"No, I was just sitting here waiting for you," replied Tommy Tipple.

"Oh?" asked Pastor Pickle, "What can I do for you?"

Swallowing the last bite of his candy bar, Tommy Tipple said, "My friend Buster Bumper told me you might be able to help me."

"Help you with what, my boy?" asked Pastor Pickle.

"Well, I want to try out for basketball at my school this fall, but I don't think I'll make the team," said Tommy Tipple with a sad look on his face.

"What makes you say that?" asked Pastor Pickle.

"I'm always the last to be picked when they choose sides for games at school. I'm clumsy and I have a hard time keeping up with everybody else in gym class. And I'm always tired. Too tired to practice and too tired to run very far."

"I know some of the kids make fun of me and say I'm fat. One boy called me Tubby Tommy to his friends. Maybe I *am* fat. Too fat to play basketball."

Pastor Pickle looked at Tommy Tipple as he considered what he had just heard.

"Well, first of all, calling people cruel names is not very kind," said Pastor Pickle as he sat down beside Tommy Tipple. "They're making fun of God's creations when they do that."

"And second," said Pastor Pickle as he looked down at Tommy Tipple's candy bar and soda, "God gave each of us the body we were born with, and it's important to him that we take good care of it. That means we need to try to keep it as healthy and as fit as possible. Sometimes our bodies become different shapes, not because that's how God designed us, but because we haven't been taking very good care of them."

"The Bible refers to our bodies as temples because this is where God lives within us," explained Pastor Pickle, pointing to himself. "I don't know about you, but I want my home for God to be as special as it can be. I want it to be as clean and strong and healthy as I can possibly make it. And to do that, you have to be intentional."

"Intentional?" asked Tommy Tipple, wide-eyed.

"Yes. You're being intentional when you decide to work on it and pay attention to it. Every day. The reason you see Doogie and me walking in Pioneer Park every morning is so we can keep our muscles exercised, our hearts and lungs working efficiently, and our brains alert and sharp."

"I've found that by exercising my mind and body and eating healthy food, I feel better and I function better throughout the day. And I'm happier! Why? Because I feel like I'm doing something good for my body. I'm being intentional about taking care of the temple God has given me."

"I guess I haven't done a very good job of being intentional," sighed Tommy Tipple, crumpling up the candy wrapper in his hand.

"Well, you can do something about that if you really want to," said Pastor Pickle. "Doogie and I are out here walking every morning at this time. Since the school year ended last week, why don't you meet us here at the fountain tomorrow morning and walk with us? We can talk more and we'll get some good exercise together."

Tommy Tipple looked up at Pastor Pickle and smiled. Then he watched Pastor Pickle and Doogie set out for their morning walk.

The next morning, as Pastor Pickle and Doogie walked from the church toward the fountain in Pioneer Park, they saw Tommy Tipple sitting on the edge of the fountain waiting for them.

"Hello, Tommy Tipple!" called Pastor Pickle as they got closer. "Good to see you this beautiful morning." He noticed that Tommy Tipple was dressed in a t-shirt, shorts and tennis shoes. "Are you ready for a workout?"

"Yes!" replied Tommy Tipple enthusiastically! "Let's go!"
"Let's go, indeed!" said Pastor Pickle as Doogie led the
way down the walking path, his tail wagging excitedly.

"How far do you and Doogie walk every morning?" asked Tommy Tipple.

"We walk all the way around Pioneer Park, from the fountain, past the playground, to the shelter house and beach on Lumpy Lake, then to the basketball court, past the merry-go-round and the amphitheater. Then we say 'good morning' to Mayor Milo Marble at his monument and finish back at the fountain."

"Wow!" exclaimed Tommy Tipple. "That's a long way. I don't know if I can go that far."

"This morning, I think we should start by just walking to the playground, okay?"

"Sounds good to me," said Tommy Tipple, who was already breathing hard and starting to feel his leg muscles twitch.

When Pastor Pickle and Tommy Tipple saw the playground come into view, they saw that Doogie was sitting beside the teeter-totter waiting for them.

Sitting down on the bench beside the walking path, Pastor Pickle said, "You did a great job, Tommy Tipple! Would you mind if we celebrate by saying a quick prayer?"

They both bowed their heads and Pastor Pickle began.

Dear God.

Thank you for this beautiful day and the opportunity to exercise our minds and bodies. We know it pleases you when we honor the life you have given us by actively looking after our health. Now we pray that you will make us a blessing to someone today. We ask these things for your glory.

Amen.

"We pushed hard today," Pastor Pickle said to Tommy Tipple as they stood up from the bench. "I had a tough time keeping up with you."

"Neither one of us could keep up with Doogie," said Tommy Tipple.

"Yeah, but Doogie cheats," said Pastor Pickle. "He has four legs. We only have two."

They laughed and Doogie ran in circles around them as they made their way back to the fountain.

The following morning Tommy Tipple was again waiting at the fountain.

Pastor Pickle sat down next to Tommy Tipple and said, "You know, exercising your body is important, but it's not the only part of being healthy. We also want to have healthy minds. And that requires exercise, too. I use my morning walk to clear my mind of things that might be bothering me."

"Really?" asked Tommy Tipple, looking puzzled. "How do you do that?"

"I turn them all over to God. I pray silently as I walk. I talk to God about things that are in my heart and on my mind. But I try not to do all the talking. I listen for what God has to say to me. It's one of the most important times of my day, when it's just God and me. No other distractions."

Pastor Pickle stood and said, "I'll tell you what. Let's agree that the first part of our walk each day... let's say from the fountain to the playground bench... will be in absolute silence. No talking to each other. Just quieting ourselves and talking silently to God."

"About what?" asked Tommy Tipple.

"It doesn't matter," said Pastor Pickle. "Just share with him whatever's on your heart. Is it a deal?"

"Deal!" said Tommy Tipple, standing up and smiling at Pastor Pickle. And this time, instead of shouting, "Let's go!" as he had the day before, he whispered to Pastor Pickle, "Let's go!"

And they did.

When Pastor Pickle and Doogie arrived at the fountain the next morning, Tommy Tipple was there with two friends, Otis Otley and Jenny June. Tommy Tipple was explaining to them about walking to the playground in silence and turning their thoughts toward God. Then, they all joined hands and Tommy Tipple whispered, "Let's go!"

And they did, as Doogie chased a butterfly down the path. They repeated this routine every morning and the walk seemed to get easier each day.

The following week, Tommy Tipple and his friends Jenny June and Otis Otley were joined by Kimberley Kite, Daren Dillow and Tara Tang. Pastor Pickle asked them if they thought they could walk a little farther and reach the shelter house at the beach at Lumpy Lake.

"Yeah, let's do it," they all agreed, standing in a circle for Tommy Tipple to whisper, "Let's go!" And then they started out, silently walking toward the playground bench where Pastor Pickle prayed and asked God to make them a blessing to someone that day.

Tommy Tipple looked up to see a beautiful rainbow shining across the sky. He pointed toward it and as the others saw it too, they looked at each other and smiled big smiles.

"Great job!" said Pastor Pickle as they arrived at the shelter house, and gave each of them a fist bump.

The following Sunday during his sermon at the
God Is Love Church, Pastor Pickle had Tommy Tipple and his
five friends stand while he told the congregation how they
had been walking together every morning.

"I am so proud of them," said Pastor Pickle with a big smile on his face. "They show up every morning ready for a workout and they're doing wonderful things to be healthier. They are following God's command to treat their bodies as temples. And they are learning to quiet themselves in the presence of God, listening for his still, small voice. I hope this is something they will continue in one way or another for the rest of their lives.

"Tommy Tipple starts each walk with an inspiring, 'Let's go!' And I think," Pastor Pickle said as he looked at each one of them, "we ought to call our group the 'Let's Go! Club."

Marcus Milkweed

Emma Eppley

Aaron Axel

Sophia Sledge

Hector Hernandez

Tara Tang

Otis Otley

Kimberly Kite

Daren Dillow

Tommy Tipple

Jenny June

On Monday morning, Pastor Pickle and Doogie were met at the fountain by an even larger group of kids which now included Tommy Tipple, Jenny June, Otis Otley, Kimberly Kite, Daren Dillow, Tara Tang, Emma Eppley, Hector Hernandez, Sophia Sledge, Aaron Axel and Marcus Milkweed. After Tommy Tipple welcomed everybody and explained the importance of the first part of the walk being in silence, they formed a large circle and whispered to each other, "Let's go!"

And down the walking path they went.

    Each morning they walked a little farther. They were now walking from the fountain to the playground bench in silence, stopping for Pastor Pickle's daily prayer asking God to make them a blessing to someone that day, then on to the shelter house at the beach on Lumpy Lake and finally to the basketball court.

At the basketball court, Tim Jimm, a senior on the Happy Hollow High School basketball team, showed them how to dribble the ball and shoot free-throws and lay-ups. They all loved it as they passed the ball back and forth.

And the group just kept growing! New members of the "Let's Go! Club" came just about every day. And they were walking farther and farther.

Another week passed and now the group walked from the fountain all the way around to the merry-go-round, where they met Anna Santana and Reese McNeece, two players on the Happy Hollow High School volleyball team.

Anna Santana led half of the group in a series of exercises including jumping jacks, squats and stretches.

Reese McNeece had the other half skipping rope. Then they switched activities.

Everybody except Doogie was laughing and breathing hard when they finished. Doogie was lying under the merry-go-round in the shade.

Toward the end of summer vacation, when the group had walked all the way to the amphitheater, Pastor Pickle had them sit down and introduced Amanda Veranda, a young lady who was attending culinary school, studying to be a chef.

"You have taken a first big step toward a healthy lifestyle by becoming active and exercising your bodies," she explained. "Please don't undo the progress you've made by eating the wrong foods."

Amanda Veranda went on to explain the basics of good nutrition and how to choose food that would benefit their health, not hurt it. She gave them written information on healthy eating that they could share with their parents and, as they left, she gave each of them a shiny red apple.

Finally it was the week before the new school year and the group walked all the way around Pioneer Park to the statue of Mayor Milo Marble, where Pastor Pickle asked them to sit down on the grass by the big monument.

MAYOR MILO MARBLE

"I just want you all to know," Pastor Pickle began, "how much Doogie and I have enjoyed walking and exercising with you this summer. Next Monday you return to school and won't be able to continue this daily walk with us. We're going to miss our time with you, right Doogie?"

Doogie barked and wagged his tail in agreement.

"Even though you won't be here each morning to walk with Doogie and me, there are lots of other ways for you to get exercise every day. Walk whenever and wherever you can. Ride your bike. Take your dog or the neighbor's dog for a walk or run. Mow the lawn or rake the leaves in your yard. Take the garbage out or help your parents in other ways with housework. Utilize opportunities to be active. Be very aware of eating right. And, whatever you do, don't forget to spend quiet time each day with God!"

"This summer you've seen what a difference all this can make in your bodies, your hearts and your minds. Doogie and I will still be walking every morning and you're all welcome to join us any time you can."

Then Pastor Pickle opened a large box and, with Tommy Tipple's help, handed out blue "Let's Go! Club" t-shirts to each one in the group.

After everyone put their shirts on, they posed for a group photo.

Pastor Pickle finished by saying, "Please keep up the good work you've started this summer! God is very proud of each of you and smiles every time you work on staying healthy. Because that's his wish for you. And remember, you're now a proud lifetime member of the 'Let's Go! Club.'"

Everyone cheered and chanted, "Let's go! Let's go! Let's go!"

Early the next morning, from inside his church office, Pastor Pickle looked up from his desk and saw Tommy Tipple walking by himself from the fountain to the bench at the playground.

When he got there, Tommy Tipple saw dozens of colorful notes taped to the bench, written by the other kids in the "Let's Go! Club." Each note thanked Tommy Tipple for getting them involved in the "Let's Go! Club" and for being a blessing to them every day.

Pastor Pickle was sure Tommy Tipple would start the new school year with a healthier body, renewed confidence, lots of new friends and a big smile on his face!

A Message From Pastor Pickle

Your health is one of the most important things you possess. Your body, full of life, is a gift from God. He wants you to treasure your health and glorify him by doing what you can to take good care of your mind and body. When you do this faithfully, you will feel better. You will have more energy. And you will be better able to accomplish the tasks you are given, by God and by others.

Taking good care of our bodies and our minds should be a lifelong priority for us all. It is something that never diminishes in importance if we want to be the very best we can be.

In the Bible, in 1 Corinthians 6:19-20, our bodies are referred to as temples. "Don't you realize that your body is the temple of the

Holy Spirit, who lives in you and was given to you by God? So you must honor God with your body."

Being intentional about getting regular exercise, eating a nutritious diet, building strong muscles and a healthy heart, and maintaining a clear, sharp mind are all ways you can thank God every day for the miracle of your life. So, as Tommy Tipple would say, " Let's Go!"

Say this prayer with me:

Dear God,
I know that life is a gift from you. Each new day is also a gift for which I am very grateful. Help me take great care of the body and mind you have given me and to remember that my body is your temple. Never let me forget that I must be very deliberate about taking good care of it every day. It's for your glory that I pray these things.

Amen.

Additional References

Don't you realize that your body is the temple of the Holy Spirit, who lives in you and was given to you by God?
1 Corinthians 6:19 (NLT)

Be still, and know that I am God! I will be honored by every nation. I will be honored throughout the world.
Psalm 46:10 (NLT)

Listen to my voice in the morning, Lord. Each morning I bring my requests to you and wait expectantly.
Psalm 5:3 (NLT)

Lead me in the right path, O Lord, or my enemies will conquer me. Make your way plain for me to follow.
Psalm 5:8 (NLT)

Pray in the Spirit at all times and on every occasion. Stay alert and be persistent in your prayers for all believers everywhere.
Ephesians 6:18 (NLT)

Made in the USA
Lexington, KY
22 March 2018